Alignment

The Shortcut to Marketplace Dominance

Rick Barrera

.

Published by Rick Barrera

PO Box 1466, Rancho Santa Fe, CA 92067

Copyright © Rick Barrera 2016

ISBN 978-0-9980736-0-6

Printed in the United States

Dedication

To my mentor, coach, client and now brother for life, Dave Zerfoss

Also to my loyal dog, Champ who sat patiently
by my side while I wrote.

Table of Contents:

Introduction

I've written this book for the impatient, pragmatic doers who want to get to the meat of this methodology as fast as possible. These hard-charging leaders just want to know how to get started and they'll take it from there. In other words, I've written this book for every serious entrepreneur, start up or business leader today. I've written this book with as much information in as few words as I feel does the concept justice. My hope is that it will help you to go forth and prosper!

My two previous books, *Overpromise and Overdeliver*, first and second editions offer many more stories, case histories and anecdotes for those who want more breadth and depth on this topic.

My clients and I learned a lot as we tried to implement the Overpromise and Overdeliver philosophy. We learned what worked and what didn't, and most importantly, where people get confused with the philosophy, the practice and the implementation. I've simplified the methodology here to make it more accessible for small businesses, online businesses, startups or any business leader that wants to take their team, department or company to the next level. It really is a very simple methodology. Most leaders want to overcomplicate it. They want to argue with the theory. They want to have a debate.

It's not that complicated. Promise your customers something they can only get from you, align your Critical Customer TouchPoints so that they amplify and reinforce your promise, and then OverDeliver on your promise. It sounds so simple…and it is, but I'll bet you can't name 10 companies that do all of the steps well.

One more thing…

There are NO perfect companies. We are all striving to get better, every day. Please understand that the companies I have used in this book are only examples to make a point and to illustrate my thinking. If they should happen to blow up in some form or fashion in the future, it does not mean the point or example is wrong. Please keep their use in context.

Please read the entire book before applying these lessons in your business. Knowing exactly where you are going will help you enormously in each of the early steps.

Chapter One: What is an Overpromise and Why Do You Need One?

Conventional wisdom says that you should under promise and over deliver, but what happens when you under promise in a crowded marketplace? NOTHING! You get no marketplace attention at all! Under promising is a one way ticket to oblivion. This is a HUGE problem. Too many companies believe that if they just deliver a good product or service that eventually, the world will discover them, and they will be successful. That is a going out of business strategy.

You must tell the world in no uncertain terms WHY they should take their valuable time to learn about you and your company and WHY they should invest their hard-earned money in your product or service. To do that you need a clearly articulated, WRITTEN Overpromise that tells the world clearly what differentiates your product or service from every other product or service on the planet. Then you need to OverDeliver on your Overpromise to KEEP your customers for life and drive viral word-of-mouth and word-of-mouse (social media).

An Overpromise is a clear articulation of what differentiates you, your company or your product or service in the marketplace.

Your OverPromise Should Score High Along Two Dimensions:

1. How radically different is your company, product or service offer from your competitors?
2. How relevant is that difference to your target audience?

I like to score each dimension on a scale from 1-10 with one being low and 10 being high as illustrated in the diagram:

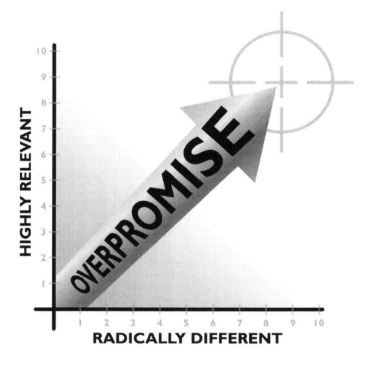

By multiplying the Different Score X the Relevant Score, you can
determine the strength of your OverPromise. For example, if you have
a Different Score of 4 and a Relevant Score of 6, you can multiply 4 x
6 for an OverPromise Score of 24. That's not very good. You are
shooting for an OverPromise Score of at least 75 to be sufficiently
motivating for potential customers to make the effort of switching to
your company and offerings.

A Great Overpromise Should Tell Your Customers:

- What to expect
- How you are different
- Why they should choose you

FedEx

When Federal Express opened its doors in 1973, why didn't they
choose as their Overpromise "WE SHIP STUFF!!!" You know the
answer. Because everyone ships stuff. There were competitors
everywhere. There were even some competitors who would ship
things overnight as part of their business. But Federal Express wanted

4

to stake out and dominate the overnight shipping space so they loudly declared **"When it absolutely, positively, has to be there overnight"** as their clearly articulated Overpromise.

What separated Federal Express from every other carrier on the planet was their complete and total focus on the overnight market. They wanted you to believe that they were the fastest shipping company on the planet. So who did they hire as their spokesman? Jon Moschitta, the world's fastest talking man. For those of you who don't know him, click here to see one of his hilarious Federal Express commercials. https://www.youtube.com/watch?v=NeK5ZjtpO-M

Other Critical TouchPoints

Call Center: Federal Express then installed special phone equipment in their call center that would actually answer the phone before it rang. What was a typical customer's reaction? "Wow, you guys are fast! The phone didn't even ring!"

Drivers: Federal Express suggested to their drivers that they put a spring in their step. They weren't to mosey to your office… they were to step lively! What impression did they give? They were FAST!

Name: Federal Express was so successful, their name became a verb, but to make it a verb that worked, their customers shortened it to FedEx as in "FedEx this to Cincinnati!" Federal Express was so in touch with their customers that they immediately shortened their legal name to FedEx.

Logo: Federal Express hired Landor Associates to redesign their logo in light of their new name. The design has won over 40 design awards and is ranked in the top 8 best corporate logos. What is miraculous is that Lindon Leader was able to create a symbol of speed within the new FedEx name and logo! He was able to incorporate a white arrow in the space between the E and the X! Talk about alignment!

The Airplane: Here is where truly great alignment thinking comes into play. FedEx had lots of choices for symbols to put into their advertising. They chose to make their symbol an airplane. Why is this so critical? Because branding wars are won in the mind as much as they are in the real world. Brands live in the mind. What was their competitor's symbol? That's right, a brown truck.

Now just imagine that your job is on the line and you absolutely, positively have to get your package there overnight! Which one would you choose? The guy with the truck or the guy with the plane? Intuitively, which one seems most likely to get your valuable package across the country in just a few short hours before your deadline? The plane of course. Alignment wins again!

In Case You Missed It, The Alignment Pattern Looks Like This:

1. **Create a clearly articulated Overpromise that differentiates you from all of your competitors. (It should score high on both the Radically Different and Highly Relevant scales in tests with customers and potential customers)**
2. **Then Overdeliver on that Overpromise at multiple customer TouchPoints to amplify and reinforce your Overpromise. This is what I call *paying off* on the promise. Another way to think about it is that you are *proving* your Overpromise to your customers at Critical Customer TouchPoints. Once they discover that you are the real deal, they will tell everyone they know.**

Here is the sad reality and the shortcut to marketplace dominance. Many companies don't deliver on their promises, or they deliver a "me too" experience. Average experiences don't drive word or mouth or viral social media. **By articulating a clear Overpromise and then consistently OverDelivering on your Overpromise, you will quickly dominate your chosen market.**

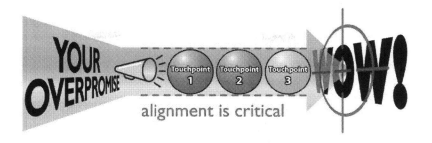

alignment is critical

The figure above shows how the Alignment process works.

Warning Number 1!

Never promise things you cannot deliver. That is not an Overpromise. It is lying! Lying will kill your company faster than Raid kills bugs! The dustbins of history are full of companies that lied to their customers. Make sure you can deliver it CONSISTENTLY AND FLAWLESSLY before you put it in your Overpromise.

Warning Number 2!

This may be the most important paragraph in the book. You must be willing to commit every resource you have to delivering on your Overpromise.

In one of the early years for Federal Express, they had a fire in one facility, a flood in another and an outage in a third. Yet, 100% of their packages were delivered on time. 100%! How many typical business leaders would have made excuses? Apologized? Blamed it on an "act of God?" Pledged to do better in the future? But not Federal Express! Why? Because they made an ironclad OverPromise to their customers that their package would "Absolutely, Positively Be There OVERNIGHT!!" They said what they meant and they meant what they said. They delivered 100% of those packages on time!

Now, let's look at where it gets really sticky. What was the cost to Federal Express to deliver on their OverPromise in the face of those three disasters? The entire year's profitability. 100% of their profits for the entire year went to ensure just 3 days of packages were delivered on time. What business leader has the guts to make that kind of call today? Not many, which is why there is so much power in actually delivering on your Overpromise. In the early years of Tesla, Elon Musk gave his personal guarantee to back the car's warrantee.

That made a powerful statement about his commitment to his customers' satisfaction. What are you willing to do for your customers?

At What Level Does the OverPromise Apply?

You can create an Overpromise for an individual product or service or for your company as a whole. You can have one for a department or a division. Ideally each product or service would have their own, but sometimes a group of products or suite of services are all designed to accomplish one thing, so in that case, there could be one OverPromise for the group or suite. Perfection is when the company's OverPromise is a summary of the product or service OverPromises beneath it. In other words your Overpromises, if you have more than one, should be Aligned. The key here is that your Overpromise should implant a single idea in the mind of your customer. Here is one more example so you can see the pattern in action.

Minute Clinic

Minute Clinic's Overpromise is implicit in their name! I love company names that declare an Overpromise! If you didn't know anything else about the company, you would have a pretty good idea of what they did. But they didn't let their marketing genius stop there. They created one of the best OverPromises of all time, **"You're Sick. We're Quick."**

What is the Typical Patient Experience When You are Sick?

Somehow, we always seem to get sick on weekends. Germs somehow know that doctors work Monday through Friday and therefore they always attack on Friday night or Saturday morning! So, you are lying on the sofa miserable until Monday morning and then you call the doctor.

The doctor's staff says they can get you in by Thursday. You'll either be well or dead by Thursday! But, you have no choice, so you agree. You go in on Thursday and sit in the waiting room where everyone else with all kinds of diseases are all coughing on you. This is what doctors call marketing. You get a new disease while you are there getting cured from your old disease! (Just kidding, but it feels true, doesn't it?)

After an eternity in the waiting room, reading the latest magazines from last year, the nurse calls you into a treatment room where you wait another eternity for the doctor to finally come in. When he does, he quickly diagnoses what is wrong with you and writes you a prescription. Feeling victorious, you pay and leave exhausted.

But you are not done. Now, you have to go to the drug store and get the prescription filled. You really don't feel like doing it now because YOU ARE SICK, but you know you need to do it to get better so you go stand in line to turn in your prescription. The friendly staff tells you it will be "about 45 minutes."

Now you have two choices. You can go home and get some much needed rest or you can wander around the store and buy stuff you don't really need. If you are like most people, you wait. This is your third eternity in a single day! If you want your life to feel really long, just get sick. Pain has a way of making time slow to a crawl.

Finally, you get your prescription, go home, take your pill and go to bed. Marathon complete.

Minute Clinic did what all truly great companies do, they saw the world through your eyes, rather than their own. They felt your pain and they came up with a great Overpromise that resonates with every sick person on the planet. "You're Sick. We're Quick."

Their OverPromise speaks directly to your immediate pain and to your contemplated pain as you think about the marathon you are going to have to run to deal with your illness the old fashioned way. They entice you to try them because they are speaking right into the heart of your deepest fear, that the old fashioned way is going to take three eternities and you just don't have the strength to deal. They are making an Overpromise that clearly tells you why they are different and why you should trust them right now. Because you are sick and they are quick and you can't think of anything more important right now than really, really fast pain relief! O.K. You got me!

"You're Sick. We're Quick," is a BRILLIANT Overpromise. But a brilliant Overpromise is a DISASTER if the organization can't deliver it. Promising things your company can't deliver is LYING! Lying to customers is the very fastest way to kill a company. So, you must be able to deliver on everything you promise, always, everywhere, consistently, and forever. In fact, as we will discuss in later chapters, you must Overdeliver to truly win customers hearts, minds and wallets. In the end, ALL brands are built on word-of-mouth and word-of-mouse (social media). Disappoint a customer and they will tell the world.

So, How Does Minute Clinic Overdeliver?

I thought you'd never ask! Minute Clinic Overdelivers through what I like to call *Critical Customer TouchPoints,* those moments of truth when your organization comes face-to-face, phone-to-phone or interface-to-interface with your customer, in other words, at the places where a customer actually makes contact with your organization.

Location and Hours of Operation: Minute Clinics (near me) are open from 9:00am to 7:30pm and on weekends from 9:00am until 5:30pm. Hours differ by location but all locations offer extended hours. There are three Minute Clinics within 5 miles of me all located inside CVS pharmacies.

Sign-in Kiosks: Minute Clinic uses electronic kiosks to gather all of your critical health and insurance data and to get signatures required from you for HIPAA Compliance. It's fast, it stores your data for future visits, it keeps costs low and it frees up the team to take care of patients.

The Disease List: Minute Clinic has a pamphlet that clearly lists the ailments they treat. If you have something not on the list, they will happily refer you to the closest facility that help you. (Pay attention to this Critical Customer TouchPoint because it is essential to Minute Clinic meeting their Overpromise. By narrowing their offer, they can be quick and effective. In other words, knowing what they don't do is as important to their model as knowing what they can do).

Diagnostic Software: Minute Clinic uses very sophisticated decision tree software to assist with patient diagnosis. At the same time it tracks what every other Minute Clinic location in the country is diagnosing in real time. This is especially helpful when local or national outbreaks or epidemics occur.

The Use of Nurse Practitioners and Physicians Assistants, Rather than Doctors: By using Nurse Practitioners and Physician Assistants, they make recruiting faster and easier, their costs are lower and they can open more locations for the same cost, which enables Minute Clinic to be closer to their patients and therefore, even quicker.

Pharmacy Co-location: One of my favorite parts of the Minute Clinic experience is the delivery of my medications. Once the Nurse Practitioner has diagnosed me with the help of their proprietary software, he or she will zap my prescription directly to the pharmacy outside the door. By the time my Minute Clinic paperwork is complete, my prescription is ready for me at the pharmacy counter!

Follow-up Calls: Two to three days after my Minute Clinic visit, I always get a follow-up call from my Nurse Practitioner, checking to see if my symptoms have abated and to offer additional assistance.

Lessons: What I want you to notice is that they entire Minute Clinic business model is built around their OverPromise. Every single TouchPoint is aligned to deliver and OverDeliver on their OverPromise.

Please also notice what they do NOT do. They don't co-locate with other doctors. They don't offer comprehensive medical treatment. They don't have fancy offices or waiting rooms with books, magazines and video games for the kids.

They have stripped the experience to the minimum required to Overdeliver on their very simple Overpromise and they have stopped there. This keeps costs low and profits high.

Aligned Innovation

I was recently waiting in a Minute Clinic when the office door opened and a nurse came out. She said that the Nurse Practitioner was busy with another patient but she would be able to get the process started in the next office. Great! I thought. This is getting even more efficient! She took my vitals and filled in the first screen of the diagnostic software and then she turned to me and asked a question. "Would you like to wait for the Nurse Practitioner or would you like to see one via our telemedicine unit? We have them standing by in remote locations to take care of backlogs. You'll just speak with him or her directly through video conference." "Sure," I said, my mind reeling with the possibilities and cost savings of this model. They could, in the future, have a centralized telemedicine center serving every CVS pharmacy with just a nurse and the telemedicine unit. They could have staff at empty clinics serving patients at busy clinics. By virtualizing staff, they can keep costs even lower and serve a larger geography even faster. Amazing…and totally aligned with their Overpromise.

Here Are Some Other Great OverPromises From Other Great Companies:

Amazon.com And You're Done.

I love this Overpromise because they were able to include their name while keeping it to just four words. It clearly describes the key benefit to buying anything and everything from Amazon. It also amplifies and reinforces the ease of use of their patented One-Click system. You start with Amazon and you are done. No three easy steps, no process needed. Just one click and your task is done. If only I could get Amazon to do my work for me in one click!

Las Vegas- "What Happens in Vegas, Stays in Vegas"

Of course this one has been parodied endlessly including the often used "What happens in Vegas ends up on the Internet." This unique Overpromise conveys a sense of mystery, fun, excitement and maybe a bit of naughtiness. OK, more than a bit of naughtiness. But it speaks directly to their target market. Those who want to break the rules…even if only for a night or a weekend.

Geico- "15 Minutes Could Save You 15% on Car Insurance"

Notice the alignment between the 15 minutes and the 15%. The call may only take 10 minutes, but by aligning the two, it sticks in the brain. You only need to remember one number for both ideas. It is fast and it saves you a significant amount of cabbage. The Overpromise has a clear benefit statement that simultaneously differentiates them from their competitors.

Lexus- "The Passionate Pursuit of Perfection"

Notice the alliteration that makes this Overpromise sticky. Notice also that they are pursuing and not arriving. They are not promising perfection, only its pursuit. This allows for model and vehicle changes while staying true to the Overpromise. They are always raising the bar on the design and quality of their automobiles but also on the entire dealership experience as well. Loaner cars are standard and dealerships have spas, clothing stores, restaurants, movie theaters, coffee bars, office spaces with Wi-Fi and more.

Apple-"Insanely Great!"

Nothing got past Steve Jobs that was not "Insanely Great!" Jobs knew that as a much smaller player in the computer industry, he had to create a dramatically better user experience to compete, so he set the threshold exceptionally high and set prices to match. By creating the coolest gadgets on the planet, he ensured that celebrities and the elite would all buy them. The rest of the world followed. Jobs really understood the power of a great Overpromise. When the iPod debuted Steve coined its Overpromise…"A thousand Songs in Your Pocket." Are you paying attention, Tim?

BMW-"The Ultimate Driving Machine"

This Overpromise is about performance but BMW didn't choose standard automotive lingo. They chose their own words that they could own, and they get special kudos for sticking with their Overpromise for four decades! There is good reason for that. It works. If you build the ultimate driving machine, what does that leave for your competitors? The super ultimate? They staked out the top position and work every day to stay there by delivering cars for people who love to drive.

USA Network- "Characters Welcome"

This is one that didn't work in the marketplace, but I personally loved. USA was a small network but they had a unique point of view. They aired showed with exceptionally well-developed but very quirky characters as their stars. Monk was the most prominent, a very quirky detective who was also very effective. Dexter, the guys from Psych and others are also "characters." It is also a double entendre inviting you, if you are a character, to join the USA Network community. I thought it was particularly clever, but apparently, it was lost on the target audience.

Kindle- Start Reading in Under a Minute

Another one from Amazon. HMMM…it seems the really good marketers are consistent OverPromisers. What is the key advantage of a Kindle book? You can have it RIGHT NOW! It's perfectly captured with Kindle's Overpromise, Start Reading in Under a Minute. It fulfils all three criteria, it tells you what to expect, how a Kindle book is different and why you should choose a Kindle book over the printed version, all in 6 words. Brilliant!

Patek Philippe- You Never Actually Own a Patek Philippe. You Merely Take Care of It For The Next Generation.

I love this Overpromise from watchmaker Patek Philippe because it simultaneously gets two points across. The first is that we've been around for generations so you can trust us, and our quality is so good that our product will be, too. Implied is that you shouldn't worry about that pesky little price tag because the cost will be spread over generations. Mere pennies a day. Patek Philippe understands that saying the word quality is useless and instead found a way to make its quality resonate with its customers by demonstrating that you are not buying a watch, but a treasured family heirloom.

What is your Overpromise? How will you grab marketplace attention with unique words that you can own in the minds of your customers? Finding exactly the right words can take research and time, but your efforts will pay off because you will be in a category of one. That is the power of Alignment and the shortcut to marketplace dominance.

In Chapter 2, I'll show you how to find your unique Overpromise.

Chapter 2

Discovering Your Overpromise

I call the process of determining your OverPromise "discovery" because you don't just randomly pick one and you will likely discover through this process that you'll want to change it to something that really resonates with your ideal customers.

It All Starts With What You Can Consistently OverDeliver

Many firms pick an Overpromise which is "aspirational," meaning that they *hope* to live up to it one day. That is a suicidal strategy. Promising things you cannot CONSISTENTLY deliver is LYING! That's why the roots of your Overpromise lie in what you are already delivering that delights your customers. If you are already in business and you have customers, you must be doing something right. They keep coming back, right?

What If I Am A New Company?

If you are a new company, you have an advantage and a disadvantage. The disadvantage is that you can't research what your customers believe you do better than anyone else. But you have an even stronger advantage in that you will be able to design your company in an aligned way right from the start. This is a huge advantage because you won't have to undo old ways of doing things and change your culture. You can do it right from the start. You'll want to start with a "working OverPromise," then design all of your Critical TouchPoints before launch. Once you've gotten things rolling, you'll want to check your assumptions and get customer feedback. Based on their feedback, you'll fine tune your TouchPoints, test your OverPromise and then launch your official OverPromise. Keep reading because you'll follow essentially the same methodology with the exception of getting to design your company right from the start.

If You Are An Existing Company...

What you need to discover is exactly what it is that your customers believe you do better than your competitors. In other words, what makes you unique and valuable in the eyes of your customers?

Why Independent Research is Critical

The problem with you asking your customers is that they often won't tell you the truth. They will tell you what they think you want to hear or say the first thing that comes to mind, but these are often not the real reasons they buy from you.

I once worked with a pharmacy chain that was growing at 15% per year but literally every one of their 169 competitive metrics was below their competitors. They asked me what I thought of their Overpromise and I told them I couldn't judge it without looking at their stores and getting some input from their customers. So, one winter day, I went and stood outside their stores and asked customers in their parking lot why they had chosen that particular drug store. Some said they had a headache and needed aspirin, others said they were picking up a prescription, still others were looking for cards or gifts.

"That's really not what I am asking," I said, "Why did you pick THIS store vs. one of their competitors." "Why did you pick this store rather than the pharmacy across the street?" In one location, they had competitors on every single corner! I really needed to know what drove them into this particular location.

"It's on the way to my office" said one. "I live right there and I'm going right there" said another. I live around the corner and this is on my way to the hairdresser, said yet another. I interviewed over 100 people at three different stores and in every single case, they chose this drug store chain because of location! Interestingly, of the 169 metrics they measured, convenient location was not among them. So, here is a company that is CONSISTENTLY superb at selecting locations, and it is REALLY important to their customers, yet they did not even measure this critical TouchPoint.

So, given what I discovered, what should their Overpromise be? Some version of convenience, of course. Sadly "convenience" is not a word that they could own because everyone uses it. They needed some clever way of saying it that would resonate with their customers. Something like "We're Right on Your Way," that would resonate when customers were thinking "Oh, I need to stop by the pharmacy! I'll go to ABC, they are right on my way." (Yes, we could
16

do better with a lot more research and wordsmithing, but alas they did not hire me for the next phase.) Why not, you ask. Because they had just launched a huge advertising campaign that focused on the superiority of their pharmacies and they felt that it would be too expensive and time consuming to change course.

Let's Look Inside

My next assignment was to investigate the soundness of their current campaign. To do so, I shopped several stores to see, if indeed, their pharmacists and the pharmacy experience (vs. the rest of the store) was indeed superior to their competitors. Sadly, I couldn't tell the difference.

In fact, when entering the store, they had set up a snakelike maze of beauty products that you had to go through to even get to the pharmacy or any other part of the store. What was truly odd about this was that their key competitor's main focus and current advertising campaign was built around beauty products! In other words, the first major TouchPoint in their stores was built on their key competitor's ad campaign! Talk about shooting yourself in the foot! That is NOT how you differentiate. It is how you get into price wars because customers can't tell the difference!

The Kernel of Truth or The Brand Essence

The bottom line is that you can't see your own company objectively and your customers often won't tell you what you really need to know. You need an independent third party and preferably a trained researcher who understands how to get to the root of what truly makes you unique. I call this finding the "Kernel of Truth," or "The Brand Essence," the one little insight into what makes your company, product or service unique. I could tell you many more stories, but they all get down to digging until you find the ONE THING that truly differentiates you from your competitors.

Questions to Ask:

1. What is the ONE THING that makes your company most unique?
2. Why did you start the company in the first place?
3. What was the founder trying to accomplish?
4. What did they believe they could change or improve about the product, industry, company or the world? What was the fundamental problem they thought they could solve that competitors couldn't?
5. Have you solved that problem yet or achieved the original vision yet? Have you cracked the code?
6. What elements of your brand or experience are most critical?
7. What three words come to mind for customers when they hear your brand or company name?
8. Why do the people who buy from you, buy from you? What keeps them from buying from competitors?
9. What keeps non-customers from buying? What do they love about your competitors?
10. What emotions are evoked by customers at each part of the purchase and use cycle?
11. How would you personify the brand? How would you personify your competitors' brands?
12. How do key stakeholders feel about your brand? What words do they use to describe it?

Identify Failure, Then Reverse It

Another key way to create differentiation is to "first identify failure and then reverse it" said Einstein. If you can find in your research something that potential customers' hate and then find a way to eliminate that pain, you are well on your way to a killer Overpromise.

How to distill the research

What you are looking for in the research is:

1. A Unique Point of View
2. A Unique Concept
3. A Unique Word or Phrase

Unique Point of View:

I was recently interviewing one of my genius colleagues for a podcast when he pointed out that the retail financial services industry is made up entirely of tacticians rather than strategists and that his belief is that all of the value is created in the strategy. Pure genius! There is a giant gaping hole of opportunity for financial advisors to position themselves as financial strategists. That point of view would be refreshing and different for their potential customers IF they could pay off on the Overpromise.

A Unique Concept:

Cold Pressed Juice is all the rage right now because, the belief goes, that they are better for you. While the health claims may be dubious, clearly the concept has caught on and the industry has grown significantly as a result of delivering a new concept to consumers that resonates with their beliefs.

A Unique Word or Phrase:

The ultimate treasure to be uncovered in your research is a unique word or phrase that you and your brand can "own." Owning the dot.com may be even more important. A phrase like "When it absolutely, positively, has to be there overnight!" is great, but what you really want is to own a single word like Volvo owns "safety" or Lexus own "luxury" for cars.

One of the coolest projects I did resulted in a phone call where a customer used the word "Impeccable" to describe the products of one of my clients. She had barely spoken the word when I instantly knew this would be the company's new Overpromise. It was a unique and unusual word that completely captured the essence of the company, their products and the brand. And just for the record, the FedEx

Overpromise also came from customer research in the form of a focus group. Never underestimate the power of great research done by the right folks.

Words That Simply Won't Work:

There are a few words that are so overused that you simply can't use them. "Quality," "service," "convenience" and "experience" are among them. They are so cliché that they simply have no meaning at all for customers. Avoid any words that others are using. Find your own word or words to own.

Make Sure You Can OverDeliver!!

Before you glom onto a point-of-view, concept, phrase or word be certain that you can OverDeliver on it CONSISTENTLY! This is my third warning on this topic in just two chapters, because one of the most common mistakes I see companies make is to claim something that they sometimes deliver or once delivered or believe that they MIGHT be able to deliver. This is DEADLY for your brand and company. It is LYING! In a world of transparency, you will be crucified for lying.

If you sometimes deliver it and know that you could deliver consistently if you really created the culture and processes around it, go for it! But make sure you are delivering it consistently BEFORE you push out your OverPromise to the public.

Now. Let's look at the initial wordsmithing, or what I call "getting it surrounded"

Chapter 3: Create Your Working OverPromise

Getting Your OverPromise "Surrounded"

I know from many years of working with clients that your deepest desire, your obsession at this point, will be to get the exact right "perfect" articulation for your OverPromise. RESIST that temptation! Your real goal at this point in the process is to just "get it surrounded." By that I mean that you will have a working definition of your OverPromise. It may be too wordy, it might even be a paragraph. It might not be the exact right words or they may not be unique, but you and your team know what you are talking about. You know what you are aiming for and your customers would recognize your "Working OverPromise." Just as a film has a "working title" during shooting, your OverPromise will be a "Working OverPromise until we get much further down the line. You'll perfect it later. You have other more important work to do right now.

Sometimes it takes weeks or months or even years to find the exact right articulation. Lexus started out with "The Relentless Pursuit of Perfection," and then after a decade changed to "The Passionate Pursuit of Perfection." Stop obsessing over the perfect articulation and instead focus on actively pursuing the rest of the process. The real magic to marketplace dominance is in completing the rest of the process, somethings most companies simply don't have the will or the discipline to complete. Separate yourself from the pack right now, by committing to the rest of the process. It will pay off in spades.

Customer Testing

Testing your OverPromise with customers and potential customers is critical. You are testing for several things:

1. Does it mean to them what we think it means?
2. Does it accurately describe our difference?
3. Does that difference matter to them?
4. Does it "resonate" with them? In other words, are they experiencing what we believed they were experiencing with other companies, products or services? Do they agree that we have significantly differentiated ourselves, our products, services, company and brand from others in our space?

5. Do they like the articulation? Would they describe it differently? How?
6. What score would they give your OverPromise? (See Chapter 1)

Market Testing

Next, you'll want to test your Working OverPromise in the different markets you serve. Different markets react differently to the same words and concepts. My last book was called *Flawless Consistency* all the way up to the week before we went to press. My editor called me with the brilliant idea to call it *OverPromise and OverDeliver*. I was kind of stunned by the idea, having lived with Flawless Consistency for over three years of writing. I wasn't really sure, but I did think it was an incredibly clever turn of phrase. With no time to test, we jumped in and made all the editorial changes and went to press.

I'm a professional speaker and a month later I presented it to my financial services clients who flatly, resoundingly, emotionally REJECTED IT! They were blown away that I would even think about telling their people to overpromise! "That is what we get sued for!" they said.

"No," I said. "You get sued because they LIE! You get sued because they promise things they CANNOT deliver, like the ability to beat the market." My logic fell on deaf ears. They wouldn't buy my book or my speech. That is what happens when you don't test. Test, test, test is the first rule of marketing. I broke it and lost. Lesson learned.

I speak in many other markets and they have all received the OverPromise and Overdeliver message with open arms. You win some, you lose some, but you always have to be moving forward. Lifelong learning is the goal!

Leaving It Alone While You Do The Rest Of The Process

Once you develop your Working OverPromise and test it to your satisfaction in the marketplace, walk away. Resist the temptation to wordsmith it to perfection at this point. What you will learn in the

OverDeliver Phase will bring hundreds or thousands more inputs that will influence your final OverPromise decision.

This happened to me recently while working on a web app for entrepreneurs, small businesses and startups to connect with each other and make deals using alternative compensation, called Partnerhere. www.PartnerHere.com Our Working OverPromise was "Unleashing Greatness" because the site was originally focused on just people matching. By the time it was built, we had expanded its capabilities so significantly that we changed the final OverPromise to "Reinventing the Way Deals Get Done."

If we had spent another 100 hours wordsmithing in the beginning, it would have all been wasted because the focus changed in the process of designing the OverDeliver. This is VERY COMMON, so don't get hung up on the final articulation right now. Get a Working OverPromise and then get very committed to the next step, truly understanding your customer's journey and the experience you want to provide because this is where the real market differentiating magic occurs.

Chapter 4: Become Your Customer

Customer Experience Mapping 101

Customer Experience Mapping can be very simple or complex. Let's start with a very simple map.

We are going to break down the customer experience into just 12 key steps or TouchPoints. A TouchPoint is any place the customer comes face-to-face, phone-to-phone or interacts in any other way with our company, products, services or people. For the purposes of this exercise, we are going to break the entire journey down into 12 or fewer TouchPoints.

Get out a sheet of paper and draw 12 boxes on it, 4 rows of three boxes. That should fit neatly on a piece of 81/2" x 11" paper. Now, in each box put one step in your customer's journey. Let's say you are a sneaker company and they are looking for a new pair of high heal sneakers. They go to Google and type in "high heel sneakers." Your site comes up first in the rankings because your SEO team is very good.

The customer then clicks on your Google organic search listing and lands on your "high heel sneakers landing page." So in the first box on your Customer Experience Map you'll put "Google high-heel sneakers." Then in the next box, you'll put "high heel sneakers landing page." Then the next box might be "click on style," followed by "click on size," etc. flowing through checkout and payment, tracking, receiving, trying on, showing friends, posting on Instagram, returning, reviewing online, repurchasing or buying a different style, disposal or donation of the used shoes, etc.

Each box gets one TouchPoint. Stay at a high level at first to ensure you can get the entire customer journey on one page.

Identifying Critical Touchpoints

Listen up, because this next piece is really critical to your success. I see companies spending MILLIONS driving themselves crazy over every single TouchPoint. (This is almost the definition of a modern corporation.) This is unnecessary and can kill your success. Perfectionism can drive a company right into the ground as fast as lying. Spreading your resources over 20 TouchPoints will increase the odds that you'll suck at all 20. Put ALL of your resources into ONE TouchPoint and you'll be world class before you know it.

There is an important balancing act here. What you are looking for are the CRITICAL Customer TouchPoints. For any given product or service or company, there are usually only 3-5 that TRULY matter to your customers. That is not to say that you can SUCK at the rest. You have to be GOOD at the rest, but you don't have to be either perfect or world class. Heck, there are entire companies built on exceling at just ONE TouchPoint. Trust me, three will give you plenty to work on.

Pick 3

The best way to keep your momentum going is to pick just 3 that you believe are <u>most critical to your customers.</u> (YES, you should TEST your theory with your customers very soon, but for now, just get with your team and pick the three you believe are MOST CRITICAL to the total customer experience.) Which TouchPoints make or break the experience from your customer's viewpoint?

Where Do We Excel, Across The Three Most Critical TouchPoints?

Is there a common theme across the three TouchPoints? Are we fast? Do we have superior expertise? Are we easier to do business with than our competitors? If so, how? Are we more tech savvy? If you can find a theme that cuts across all three TouchPoints you'll be ahead of the game but it is not critical at this juncture. Your theme may or may not be the same as your Working OverPromise.

Find Your Point of View

Now is a good time to consider your unique point-of-view. Do you have a POV that cuts across all three TouchPoints? Are you trying to save your customers money? Are you trying to change the industry in some way? Are you trying to build a sustainable world? Are you anti-establishment? Are you trying to bring transparency to a non-transparent space? If you can articulate your unique POV, it will make the next steps easier as you work to amplify and reinforce your TouchPoints in the next section.

Chapter 5: Three TouchPoints Make a Brand

One of my favorite sayings is that "Three TouchPoints Makes a Brand," by which I mean that you can build a globally differentiated brand by differentiating just three TouchPoints, IF...pay attention now, those three TouchPoints are ALIGNED! Just as Minute Clinic aligned around "quick" and FedEx aligned around "overnight," you can build a globally differentiated brand by differentiating just three TouchPoints... as long as your differentiation is aligned around a single idea or theme.

Amplify and Reinforce TouchPoint One

Pick one of your Critical TouchPoints and put it on steroids. Make it AMPLIFY AND REINFORCE your Overpromise. If you are fast, make this TouchPoint faster, if you are easy, make this TouchPoint easier, if you are sustainable, make this TouchPoint super-sustainable.

What I mean by amplify is that you make this TouchPoint bigger, more pronounced, more obvious than it was before. What I mean by reinforce is that this TouchPoint picks up the theme of your OverPromise and reinforces your OverPromise message.

This is where the real work begins and where most companies fail. They fail because they believe what they are doing is good enough. They fail because they believe that five or ten percent better is enough to differentiate them in the marketplace. They fail because they don't understand how different you have to be in today's marketplace to grab attention, PR and legions of new raving fans. They think good enough is good enough. It isn't.

Vanilla is Taken

To quote the brilliant marketer Seth Goden, "Vanilla is taken." You must take your customers' experience at your Critical TouchPoint to the extreme. Amazon did this with "One-Click" ordering. They even patented it so others can't use it or must pay a royalty to do so. How do you beat "One-Click?"

Zero clicks? Yes! That's why Amazon introduced automatic ordering so you receive your stuff every month without even having to "One-Click."

Amazon took it to an extreme and now they are once again beating themselves at their own game. With the Echo, you can now speak your order and not even click once! That is taking a TouchPoint to an extreme! Think world class, not just "better."

Strategies for Rocking Your TouchPoints:

- Name it- Give it a cool name that highlights its uniqueness for your customers

- Color it- Change its color to make it more noticeable

- Package it- How can you wrap it uniquely?

- Amplify it- How can you make it dramatically more pronounced?

- Connect it- What can you connect it to that would make it cooler?

- Reinforce it- How can you remind your customers that this is the payoff of your OverPromise?

- Exaggerate it- Be gutsy here!

- Provide more of it- If a little is good…

- Take it to the next level- What would represent a breakthrough? What would be unexpected?

- Push it to the ridiculous- Stop holding yourself back…How far can you go? If you think your idea is crazy, you are just warming up…

- Make it more of whatever it already is- If it's hot, make it hotter, if it's cool, make it cooler, if it's sexy, make it sexier!

- Demonstrate its uniqueness- SHOW ME what is so unique about it!

- Show me a video- How should I use it to rock my world?

- Educate me- on what I don't understand that makes this TouchPoint SOOOO cool!

- Illustrate the difference- Visuals are incredibly important. SHOW ME!

- Make the invisible visible- How can you make something I can't see, something I can see?

- Show me the ROI using my metrics- Get into my head and show me why I can't live without this and how my return will be tenfold my investment.

Align it with other Critical TouchPoints- Above all, make sure it is aligned around your OverPromise and aligned with all Critical TouchPoints.

Invest More Time and Money in Fewer TouchPoints

This is another concept foreign to most companies. They love to spread their limited investment dollars over multiple projects. They believe they are "hedging their bets" or "attacking on multiple fronts" but in reality what they are doing is ensuring failure.

When Steve Jobs decided to get into the music business, he built iTunes in 9 months. Apple had never been in the music business before and didn't have a single contract for access to the record labels' music catalogs. They had no design for a retail music portal. Yet in 9 months iTunes was open to the public. Nine months later Apple did it again with "A Thousand Songs in Your Pocket" via the iPod, a portable music device Apple built from scratch with suppliers, components and processes they had never used. How did they do these seemingly miraculous things? Focus. Focus. Focus. The entire organization was focused on ONE project for 9 months and they COMPLETED the project. Then they did it again. Pay attention. This is the real genius of Apple. What if you worked on just one TouchPoint this year…and got it exactly right? How would your world change? I'll wager that it would rock your customers' world…and your bottom line.

Chapter 6: Lather, Rinse, Repeat

Amplify and Reinforce TouchPoint Two

Now that you have amplified and reinforced one TouchPoint, it's time to do it again. Choose the second TouchPoint that you believe will most impact your customer's experience.

Take It to an Extreme

Sommerset builds high-end customized houseboats. Customers come to their factory to design the boat of their dreams. Then, they have to come back to the factory several times during the construction to sign off on each stage of completion and because they are excited about their boat and want to see how it's coming along.

The sommerset team decided it would be cool to post daily pictures of each boat's progress online so the customers could see their dreams being built. The response was overwhelming! People were so excited about their boats that they wanted to show them to their friends but because the site was password protected, they had to give their login information to their friends. That really wasn't secure or practical. They asked Sommerset to solve the problem.

Rather than post each boat by the owner's name, Sommerset gave each boat a number. Then all pictures were posted on a public site. Now all owners had to do was give their friends their boat number and their friends could follow the excitement of the build. The pictures also served as an idea board, long before Pinterest, inspiring other owners for their builds.

Well, as you might guess, the boards led to their friends getting so involved that they often decided to build a boat of their own. That, in turn led to the creation of Sommerset boating communities and to the launch of several regattas sponsored by Sommerset.

As owners decided to upgrade, they asked Sommerset what to do with their old boats. Sommerset posted them on the picture site and soon got into the used boat business. Next, owners said it was hard to find insurance for their boats, so Sommerset got into the houseboat insurance business.

Sommerset wasn't afraid to take their offerings to an extreme to keep their customers happy. Their exceptional handling and redesign of one Critical TouchPoint led them into businesses and industries they were not familiar with. Yet, they boldly went where no houseboat company had gone before, and they were handsomely rewarded.

Align and Connect TouchPoint One and Two

Make sure that after you have amplified and reinforced TouchPoint Two to go back and make sure it is still aligned with your OverPromise and TouchPoint One. If it isn't, don't panic. Take another look at your theme and your TouchPoints. Is it time to change the theme to something that better represents your new and improved TouchPoints? Or can you adjust something to better reflect your theme?

Also look to see if you can connect TouchPoint One and TouchPoint Two. Is there a way to make the connection stronger with naming conventions, colors, styles or other kinds of connective tissue?

In Chapter 7 we'll get into look at how to drive emotional connection with your Critical TouchPoints.

Chapter 7: Shifting Emotions

Amplify and Reinforce TouchPoint Three

You're on a roll. Two TouchPoints down. You are ready to take on TouchPoint Three! So let's take it up a notch. For TouchPoint Three let's focus on the EMOTION you want to create for your customers at that TouchPoint. Emotion is essential for every TouchPoint. As "producers," we have a tendency to think about each TouchPoint from our point of view. When using the Alignment Methodology, it is important that we think about each TouchPoint from the customers' point of view. I hope you have been doing that all along, but for this TouchPoint, let's really focus on the customer's emotions. What are they feeling before they get to this TouchPoint, <u>what are we doing to change their emotion</u> at this TouchPoint, and what emotion are they feeling as they "leave" this TouchPoint. In other words, this TouchPoint, like all TouchPoints, should elicit an emotional reaction of some type.

Fast and Slow, Up and Down

The goal of shifting emotions is the shift itself. Starbucks is designed to give you a jolt, a spa is designed to chill you out. Sporting events rev your engine and speed you up, fine dining and a nice glass of wine slow you down.

Some TouchPoints feel "efficient." I was in the Toronto airport last week and was quite impressed with the way they used integrated technology at every step to both speed my journey AND track my every movement. The message was clear. "Don't try anything here, buddy, because we've got you covered including fingerprints, photos and video. But, that in no way should interfere with your first class travel experience or speed through our airport. Have a nice day!"

Some TouchPoint feel "thorough," like when a triage nurse checks you into the emergency room or a financial advisor screens your suitability for his advice. But these TouchPoints can also feel "clinical" or "uncaring", or "bureaucratic" or "stand-offish." Is that the way you want them to feel? What will you do to change the way they feel?

Every TouchPoint Feels Like Something!

My point is that every TouchPoint feels like something and it is <u>what we do *to* customers and *with* customers that changes the way they feel</u> about each TouchPoint. How they feel and how their feelings are changed at each TouchPoint is what managing the customer experience is all about. What do each of your TouchPoints feel like? What do you want them to feel like? <u>What will you say and do to change the way your customers feel at each TouchPoint?</u> How will what your customer sees and what you say and do at each TouchPoint amplify and reinforce your OverPromise?

Taking It to an Extreme

American Girl Place is an extreme adventure for girls. This Ultra-TouchPoint Extravaganza is the perfect demonstration of Alignment on steroids. American Girl Place is one of the offerings from American Girl Dolls, where each doll is "born" with a "story." Ashlyn, and Kendall and Kaya and Josefina and their friends all come with a backstory and a host of accessories and books about them that are all true to their heritage and time period, which are some pretty cool TouchPoints to begin with.

American Girl Place just blows the doors off their competition with an all-day adventure that includes a 150 seat theater where you can watch "your doll and her friends" acting out exciting and sometimes educational parts of their lives. Then you and your doll can stroll the fashion runway, just like real fashion models in the fashions of your choice while the paparazzi (AKA, your parents) flash away.

If you work up an appetite, you and your doll can be seated in the café where your doll will sit in a doll sized seat and order doll sized food to go on the doll sized tableware. Then you can retire to the beauty salon where you and your doll can sit side by side and get identical hairdos, which demands, of course, a photo shoot with the photographer!

Each of these TouchPoints is designed to deliver delight, excitement, relaxation, respite, wonder, more excitement and more delight followed of course by good old fashioned exhaustion and contentment. But please note that these TouchPoints are orchestrated

36

to create a full-day of emotional events. Not one of them happens by accident. Each part of the American Girl adventure is designed, staged and choreographed to deliver one delighted little girl after another out the door at the end of the day. This is what brilliant Alignment looks like, sounds like and feels like in practice. If you have never been to American Girl Place, have a daughter or borrow one and watch this extraordinary adventure unfold before your eyes. They are masters of Alignment.

Check All TouchPoints for Emotional Impact

Now that you understand how important emotion and changing emotion is, go back to each of your Critical TouchPoints and check to see if the emotion you are creating is the emotion you want to create. If not, take the time now to redesign that TouchPoint.

It Time to Connect and Align All Three TouchPoints

Now is the time to revisit all three of your TouchPoints to ensure that each of them is aligned with your theme. Or to adjust your theme, now that you have perfected each of your Three Critical TouchPoints. Or maybe you've discovered that one of your TouchPoints isn't really that critical and perhaps there is another you should have included.

Do You Have the Right Theme?

Make whatever adjustments you need to make to your theme and TouchPoints to ensure the tightest alignment possible across your TouchPoints, because we are going to pick up the pace of implementation from here. Take one last look and if there is ANYTHING that doesn't feel quite right, address it now. Make sure that you are feeling rock solid that these three TouchPoints will blow your customers' minds when you roll them all out together.

Chapter 8: OverDeliver

You'll probably recall that we said we were going to OverPromise AND OverDeliver. So now is a great time to check and see if we are in fact, OverDelivering for our customers.

There are Two Levels of OverDelivering:

Level 1-Delivering more, better or differently than our competitors at each of our critical TouchPoints.
Level 2- Delivering Something Extra ^{TM} **that our customers don't expect as part of our core offering.**

Check Your Experience Against Competitors
Now that you have designed your Three TouchPoint Experience, check out your competitors experience to ensure that *your customers' experience* is in fact different and significantly better. I would again urge you to use an independent third party to evaluate all experiences. It is hard to be objective when it is your company, product, service or experience. Hire someone who is not afraid to tell you the truth. It will cost you much less to fix it now than after you deploy.

Check for Relevance!
If you remember the formula for a great OverPromise, it is Differentiation X Relevance. So, now that you've checked to see how different your TouchPoints are vs. your competitors, it's time to check for Relevance. Again, make sure you are getting unbiased feedback on how relevant your differentiated TouchPoints are to your current and potential customers.

Something Extra™

What if you could surprise and delight your customers with a little Something Extra™ each time they interact with you?

My wife owns a catering company called ***Something Homemade.*** It's called Something Homemade because, amazingly, everything is

homemade, from scratch, including all sauces, dips, condiments, garnishes and dressings. (Yes, she is a very serious chef.)
After each event she caters, her team cleans the kitchen, leaving it spotless…except for one small thing.

She always makes a little Something Extra™ for the hosts to enjoy the next day. It might be a loaf of homemade banana bread, a bag of homemade cookies or a basket of breakfast scones with homemade jam or it might be an entire meal for the day after a wedding reception. It's always different and always tailored to her customer's situation and favorite foods. It's a sweet way to say thank you for the business and it ensures an always positive final TouchPoint.

You Can Do It, Too
Some companies drop gifts, candy or gift cards into their shipping boxes. This serves two purposes. It ensures that the person who opens the box is thorough in emptying the box and it is a little surprise that makes their day a little brighter. It also serves as a final reminder of why they should buy from your company again.

The Blue Tiffany Box might just be worth more than what is inside. Why? Because of the anticipation it builds by its very presence. Women respond very predictably to the little blue box because it heralds the company's reputation for delivering high-end jewelry that delights. It also speaks volumes about the thought and care the purchaser has put into to ensuring that something special is in store for you.

American Airlines Frequent Flyer Miles started out as something extra and became the tail that wagged to dog. No serious flyer would consider buying an airline ticket today without considering the interplay of miles and benefits.

Patagonia and Zippo lighters (made in my hometown of Bradford, PA) both offer lifetime warranty's on their products. You can skid down Mount Everest on your back and Patagonia will repair your jacket for free. You can use your Zippo lighter as a screwdriver, hammer and knife (as one Viet Nam Veteran did) and Zippo will repair it for free. I'd say that's a pretty valuable Something Extra.™

Amazon Prime started out as something extra and became its own product. Prime was originally a way to get customers to opt in and subsidize the cost of two-day shipping. For $79 per year, you could get unlimited two-day shipping on "Prime Eligible" items for a year. It was a screaming deal for people like me who tap their Amazon mouse like a starving gerbil.

But Then It Got Really Interesting...

Amazon added video streaming services to Prime with over 5000 television shows and movies to choose from. Then they added streaming music. And then the floodgates opened...

- **FREE Two-Day Shipping** on eligible items to addresses in the contiguous U.S. and other shipping benefits. For more information, go to Amazon Prime Shipping Benefits.
- **FREE Same-Day Delivery** in eligible zip codes. For more information, go to Order with Prime FREE Same-Day Delivery.
- **Prime Now:** Get FREE two-hour delivery or scheduled delivery on over 10,000 items, from groceries to electronics and more. Plus, get free delivery from your favorite local stores. Available in eligible zip codes only. For more information go to Prime Now.
- **Restaurant Delivery:** Get FREE one-hour delivery from popular restaurants with Prime Now. Available in eligible zip codes only. For more information, go to Prime Now.
- **Prime Video:** unlimited streaming of movies and TV episodes for paid or free trial members in the U.S. and Puerto Rico. For more information, go to About Prime Video.
- **Prime Music:** unlimited, ad-free access to hundreds of Prime Playlists and more than a million songs for members in the U.S. and Puerto Rico. For more information, go to About Prime Music.
- **Prime Photos:** Secure unlimited photo storage in Amazon Cloud Drive. For more information, go to About Prime Photos.
- **Prime Pantry:** Access to Prime Pantry, where members can purchase and ship to addresses in the contiguous U.S. low priced grocery, household, and pet care items for a flat delivery fee of $5.99 for each Prime Pantry box. Prime Pantry orders cannot be shipped to addresses in Alaska, Hawaii, and Puerto Rico.

- **Amazon Elements**: Access to <u>Amazon Elements</u> products, Amazon's own line of everyday essentials.
- **Amazon Dash for Prime**: Never run out of your favorite products with Amazon Dash Button. For more information, go to <u>Amazon Dash Button</u>.
- **Prime Early Access**: Get 30-minute early access to Lightning Deals on Amazon.com and new events on MyHabit.com. For more information, go to <u>About Prime Early Access</u>.
- **Kindle Owners' Lending Library**: access to members in the U.S. For more information, go to<u>Kindle Owners' Lending Library</u>
- **Kindle First**: Early access for members in the U.S. to download a new book for free every month from the Kindle First picks. For more information, go to <u>Kindle First</u>.
- **Video Add-On Subscriptions**: Members can purchase Video Add-on Subscriptions to premium content providers. <u>Browse available Video Add-on Subscriptions,</u> or <u>manage your existing subscriptions</u>.
- **Deals and Discounts, Compliments of Amazon Family:** These include 20% off diapers through Subscribe & Save and 15% off eligible products from your baby registry. For more information go to <u>Get 20% off Diaper Subscriptions</u> or <u>About the Completion Discount</u>.
- **Prime Exclusive Savings in Video Games:** Members in the U.S. save 20% on new release physical video games during pre-order through two weeks after launch. For more information, go to<u>Prime Exclusive Savings in Video Games</u>.
- **Membership Sharing**: Two adults living in the same household can create an Amazon Household to share certain Amazon Prime benefits. For more information, go to <u>About Amazon Households</u>.

SHEEEZZZEEE…Talk about taking it to the extreme!!!

TEST, TEST, TEST!

It's time to market test each of your Three Critical TouchPoints. If you haven't already rolled them out to beta groups, key clients or your whole customer base, this is the time to do it. Role them out one at a time, testing customer responses as you go. If you get significant negative feedback, go back to the drawing board or do a deep dive with those customers who are screaming the loudest. They probably have exactly the insights you are looking for that will represent a breakthrough at a Critical TouchPoint.

If you are getting good feedback, keep rolling them out and tweaking them until you are delivering flawlessly and you are getting consistently positive responses from your customers. This is the hardest part of the entire methodology so don't lose heart. This is what will separate you from the pack and be the foundation of your marketing and differentiation efforts going forward. Take the time to get it exactly right before you announce your OverPromise.

Chapter 9: Bringing It All Together!

Revisit Your Overpromise

Now, it's time to revisit your Overpromise. Does your Working OverPromise still align with your new and improved Critical TouchPoints? Is it the best articulation for your new TouchPoints? Hopefully, you've already had an epiphany as you pushed and pulled on your Critical TouchPoints. Hopefully, you've accidentally tripped across the perfect phraseology in your work with your customers designing and delivering your new TouchPoints.

Now, Man. Do It Now!

Now is the time to ensure <u>Perfect Alignment</u> of your OverPromise with your Three Critical TouchPoints. Take the time now to get it exactly right. NOW is the time to obsess over the <u>perfect wording</u> for your OverPromise. If you and your team can't get the articulation exactly right, now is the time to hire a wordsmith or marketing coach to help you.

Customer Testing

This testing is critical. You need to make sure that your words mean the same things to customers that they mean to you. You need to make sure they invoke the same emotions that you intended. You need to make sure that they understand how you are differentiated in the marketplace.

In one of the most famous marketing blunders ever, Chevrolet launched their premier mid-sized sedan into Mexico spending millions of pesos in advertising without ever testing. It was a colossal flop. After all why would anyone ever buy a car called a Nova? In Spanish, it means "Doesn't go!"

Plug-in Hybrids are having the same issue today. I understand what an electric car does. I understand what a hybrid does. But why would spend the time and money to install a giant charging station in my garage and then pay extra for a plug-in hybrid to go 12 miles on a charge when I'm already getting 40 miles to the gallon in my hybrid?

Get Testimonials

During your tests, you'll have a great opportunity to get on camera (or audio or written) testimonials! If your customers are loving the new you, what a perfect time to capture their excitement to share with others! Let them tell your new story about how cool and Aligned your new company is!

Market Test

Ok, you've tested with your customers who apparently already love you or at least like you, because they are still doing business with you. Now it's time to roll out to potential customers and competitors customers to see how they respond. Resist the temptation to explain yourself or "sell" your new TouchPoints. Let your experience, marketing materials or website do the work and see if they "get it." If they don't, your model may not be scalable. Test, test, test and fine-tune your messaging until they can grasp it quickly.

Tighten Your Messaging Around Your New Business Model

Assuming that your market testing is positive, it's time to revisit each of your communication channels to ensure that you messaging is completely aligned across every channel.

Make sure your website is telling the story of your uniqueness, clearly and prominently displaying your new OverPromise on every page. Make sure that you clearly spell out how you OverDeliver on your OverPromise. Make sure the graphics match. Check to see that there are no conflicting messages that might confuse potential buyers.

Brochures and printed materials must be reviewed to ensure that they are amplifying and reinforcing your OverPromise. Sales presentations must be updated. Trade show booths should be reinvented to bring your story and your OverPromise to life with interactive demos or video or other engagement tools. Your "On-Hold" messaging should reflect your new OverPromise. Walk around your office and ask yourself if your new OverPromise would be obvious to anyone who walked in. If not, it's time for a change. Review your interview answers for radio or television appearances. Check every potential communications TouchPoint to ensure that your messaging is completely Aligned.

Now it's getting exciting! You're ready to launch your new OverPromise into the world!

Chapter Ten: Getting Ready to Launch Your New Overpromise

The Launch!

You've done a lot of hard work. You've gotten your TouchPoints aligned and perfected, you are ready to OverDeliver and you know exactly what your New OverPromise is. You are ready to announce to the world what you stand for and how exactly they will benefit by being your customer.

Whip The Team Into A Frenzy!

The Launch Rally- If your internal team is not sold on your New OverPromise and your new super-cool TouchPoints for OverDelivering, your customers will never get excited. Now is the time to roll out your new program internally to every employee. Make sure they ALL know exactly what your message is, how it works and <u>why it is so important to customers to receive this level of service consistently.</u> Make sure they clearly understand their role in OverDelivering.

Make sure they understand all of your new messaging, including your website, brochures, social media, email campaigns, talking points, sales presentations, signage and all the other promotional materials that are available for their use.

Customers will be asking them about the new messaging and what it means. Make sure everyone understands the entire process. It is critical that they understand that they must LIVE THE BRAND every day with every customer with every interaction.

Turn Up the Volume

Now is the time to ensure that the world knows who you are and what you stand for. You've been in stealth mode up until now, testing and perfecting. Now is the time to turn up the volume on all of your messaging to all of your stakeholders and anyone else in the community who will listen. Now is the time to launch your PR campaign and invite the press to see what you are doing.

Launch Event(s)

Now is the time to have a launch party for your new OverPromise and your new customer focused TouchPoints. Invite influential customers, potential customers, press, key influencers, friends and family. Your launch party is the time to release your inner Steve Jobs. Get on stage and tell the world how awesome your company and team are!

Do Something Crazy that Amplifies Your Message

Donald Trump is a master at getting free publicity. By the time you read this he might even be president! How can you do something crazy that will amplify your message and get you some free publicity? Don't be afraid to be outrageous! Just don't be offensive.

If you haven't read Guerrilla PR 2.0 by Michael Levine, you need to do so right now. https://www.amazon.com/Guerrilla-P-R-2-0-Effective-Publicity/dp/0061438529

The moment you finish that book, you need to read Newsjacking by David Meerman Scott. https://www.amazon.com/Newsjacking-Inject-Breaking-Generate-Coverage-ebook/dp/B0065MKMMS#nav-subnav

Turn up the Frequency

You've been living with your new OverPromise and developing and perfecting your TouchPoints for a long time… weeks, months or even years in some cases. You are probably sick of talking about them. But your public hasn't heard anything about them. They've been going about the business of living their lives or running their companies. They have really not been paying much attention to you at all. **HEAR THIS… It is virtually impossible to Over Communicate your OverPromise.**

You need to be communicating your new OverPromise EVERYWHERE, at every customer TouchPoint, every day, and every transaction. You have to SELL your story! Every employee must be telling your new story in every communication.

Turn up the Reach

Reach is an advertising term that means the NUMBER of people who hear your message. Now is the time to reach out to all those past customers, non-customers and potential customers so you can tell them your story. Sell them on your OverPromise and how you OverDeliver like no one else in the industry. Create AN IRRESISTIBLE OFFER to get them to try you out and see for themselves how awesome you are. Find others with lists of the companies or people you want as your customers and partner with them to reach even further.

Get your Suppliers Involved

When you win, your suppliers win. Make sure you get them on board with how awesome your new OverPromise is and show them exactly how they can partner with you to help your company grow, which means more business for them.

Get Your Customers Involved

Your best customers should be among those who have already received the benefits of your new and improved TouchPoints and they should be willing to tell others about how awesome you are. Get video testimonials or written testimonials you can use in your marketing and social media. Use them as reference accounts. Ask for referrals. Ask them to partner with you in growing your company so you can afford to do even more cool things for them in the future. Get them involved in figuring out the next TouchPoint that you should add, change or improve.

Hammer Your Social Media

You need to hammer your message home using every social media tool you can master as often as possible to get your message out. Tell your story and keep telling your story to anyone who will listen.

Know This...

Most companies change their ad campaigns every 12-18 months, yet research shows that it takes customers and potential customers almost 10 years to fully absorb your message and "get" who you are and what differentiates you from competitors. Stay on message until your customers can recite your OverPromise forward and backward. That will most likely be measured in decades...

Chapter Eleven: Reaping the Rewards

Reap the Rewards of Your New Business Model

Now, you should be reaping the rewards of your New OverPromise and its impact on your bottom line. Sales should be up and your sales and marketing people should be seeing and measuring increased awareness and preference for your brand and company and your products and services. Sales cycles should be shorter and customers should be happier. Cash flow should be up and your profits should be fatter. Well done! What's next?

Turn Up The Volume On Your Existing TouchPoints

Now that you are pushing volume through your Three Critical TouchPoints, you should be finding ways to make them even cooler and more differentiated. You should be collecting customer feedback on each TouchPoint and how it impacts the overall customer experience. Customers should be telling you what would be even more valuable.

A few years ago, I was working with an equipment rental company and we had this idea that if we had a mobile unit that could park right on their job site, that we would be their preferred vendor. We turned out to be right. Almost immediately, they gave us most of their business.

But within 60 days they came back with a request. Having the office on site was really helpful, but they did most of their planning for their requirements at night. Would it be possible for us to join them at the end of their meetings, they asked? That way we would be hours ahead of their actual needs and could have everything in place on ALL of their job sites BEFORE they began work for the day. They went on to say that if we did that, there really wouldn't be a need for us to have the mobile unit on site.

This was a huge win for us because we could lower our costs while earning all of their business. We had our units on site before our competitors got out of bed! They helped us design that TouchPoint in a way that worked perfectly for them and was hugely profitable for us. Never stop tweaking your Critical TouchPoints to serve your customers better!

Add Another TouchPoint

Things should be settling in for you operationally by now, so that means it's time to add a Fourth Critical TouchPoint. You know they drill. You know how to find it and what to do with it. When you get that one in place, look for one more. Five Aligned TouchPoints will put you at the top of your field in any industry.

Start Over

I know you want to sit back and watch the cash roll in, but your competitors are stinging from the business you took from them and you need to up your game. When you have completed the redesign of Five Critical TouchPoints, start over from the beginning to make sure that your big five are the same as your customers big five. Technology, competitors and customers are always changing. You have to keep changing too, if you want to stay on top.

Look for Opportunities to Leverage Technology or Eliminate the TouchPoint

Often, when you are redesigning a TouchPoint, you realize that:

- You can replace that TouchPoint with technology
- You can eliminate the TouchPoint altogether

Never be afraid to deploy technology to lower your costs and serve your customers better. If you don't do it, your competitors will. Just make sure that it actually serves the customer better. You should also constantly be asking yourself if this TouchPoint is necessary at all.

For years, I've been asking the hotel industry why I have to check in. They know when I am coming, they have my credit card from the reservation, and keys could easily be mailed to me in advance or picked up at a kiosk. Finally, this is becoming a reality at some hotels. That doesn't mean eliminating the front desk. It just means a shift in their function and their ability to do what humans do best, be friendly, solve unique problems and add value in ways that only humans can.

Synthetic oils eliminated 50% of oil changes. Remember, if you don't do it, your competitors will.

Many years ago, Xerox focused on building the best copier repair service in the industry. Meanwhile, their competitors built machines that needed far less service. Guess who won?

Chapter 12: Three Types of TouchPoints

I put this chapter last because I didn't want to confuse you. We've been talking about Aligning your Three Critical TouchPoints. What I want to talk about here is three different TYPES of TouchPoints. Each TYPE has strategic implications so knowing about them and using them strategically can have huge advantages.

If you would like a really deep dive into the three types along with case studies for each, please pick up a copy of either or both editions of my previous books entitled "Overpromise and Overdeliver." You can get both at https://www.amazon.com/s/ref=nb_sb_ss_c_2_11?url=search-alias%3Dstripbooks&field-keywords=overpromise+and+overdeliver&sprefix=overpromise%2Caps%2C196

Product TouchPoints

Product TouchPoints are any TouchPoint that the customer gets to keep. That includes the product itself, like a car, house or computer. But it also includes things like brochures, packaging, supplies and even invoices.

Examples of Product and Service TouchPoints include:

- Brochures and advertising
- Stationery
- Mail and Email
- Ease of obtaining information about the category, your product and competitive products
- Product reviews from customers and independent 3rd parties
- Product availability
- Size
- Color
- Feature set

- Sales proposals
- Ease of purchase
- Types of credit accepted
- Financing
- Warranties
- Forms
- Invoices
- Contracts
- Ease of parking
- Ease of installation
- Documentation
- After sales service
- Parts availability
- Usage information
- Who else uses your product
- Packaging
- Shipping methods
- Recyclability
- Complementary product information
- Accurate real time information on order and delivery status
- Access to your network
- Value added services
- Education
- Company or plant tours
- And lots more!

Systems TouchPoints

Systems TouchPoints are anything the customer touches but does NOT get to keep. This includes things like your retail store, website, and kiosk or hotel room.

Examples of Systems TouchPoints Include:

- Telephone interface
- Fax interfaces
- Web interfaces
- Kiosks
- Customer facing software
- Offices
- Signage
- The speed with which you answer the phone
- Your telephone greeting
- Your customer interviewing methodology
- Your sales methodology
- Your process for working a referral
- Voice mail message
- Cell phone message
- Your vehicles
- Your cycle time
- Your follow-up system
- Customer surveys
- Any other systems or processes that touch the customer

Human TouchPoints

Human TouchPoints are anywhere your team comes face-to-face, phone-to-phone or chat-to-chat with your customers. Human TouchPoints includes all human-to-human interaction.

Why Bother?

Why do I bother to make this distinction about TYPES of TouchPoints? Because this is where you can really be strategic in your thinking about how to differentiate your company and brand from your competitors. This is where you can zig where they zag. And because each of these different types of TouchPoints has its own uniqueness that will impact you monetarily and operationally.

Amazon is a perfect example of a company that strives to have NO human TouchPoints at all. Why? Because operationally, you will always have the most variation at the Human TouchPoint. Amazon is built on the premise of self-service with a very sophisticated user interface that DESIGNS OUT the need for Human TouchPoints. Given their success, I'd say they are doing that very well.

Four Seasons Hotels, on the other hand, is designed around the Human TouchPoint. They have a 4:1 staff to guest ratio which means there is always someone at hand to take care of your every whim. It also means that operationally speaking, recruiting and training is a huge focus and a huge part of their costs. Leadership is critical. But because they have built an extraordinary culture of human to human service, their reputation allows them to charge some of the highest room rates in the industry.

Apple's iPhone was a Product TouchPoint that was so superior to its rivals when it launched that all of the other TouchPoints paled in comparison. Because the iPhone was exclusive to AT&T, 40% of initial iPhone customers switched wireless companies to get an iPhone. In other words, they traded down to an inferior network (systems TouchPoint) to get a superior Product TouchPoint. Two years later when the iPhone contract with AT&T ran out, they switched back to their better networks while keeping their iPhones.

When I originally made the distinction in types of TouchPoints, it was because most companies are really good at one of the types and simply ignore the others. It's OK to ignore or downplay one or more types of TouchPoints if you are superior at one, but at least do so BY DESIGN. Never ignore a TouchPoint or a type of TouchPoint by accident. Having the greatest widget on the planet is not useful if your website sucks so badly that I give up before I buy it or discover after I buy it that I can't easily get parts, service or supplies. Being difficult to do business with will always kill you in the end. Know how critical (or not) your Human TouchPoints are because it will dictate how you recruit, onboard, train and coach your teams.

<u>Be aware of the design you are creating and use your TouchPoints and the different types of TouchPoints strategically.</u> Do honest research and know where you have strength and weakness. There are no perfect companies on the planet, so don't despair. Just play to your strengths strategically and be aware of those TouchPoints and types of TouchPoints you need to address to be a world class competitor.

Something Extra ^{TM} for You

I have to practice what I preach so here is a little Something Extra ^{TM} for you. Here are three ideas that will make your OverPromise soar.

Recruit to Your Brand

I've mentioned that the Human TouchPoint is the most variable because of the natural variation in human beings, but each of us has patterns of behavior that will be more or less compatible with a particular culture.

Southwest Airlines hires people who love people. Their thinking is that when you take 300 strangers and put them in aluminum tube five miles in the air, you better hope they all get along. Their flight attendants are the lubrication that makes sure they do. They all love being around people. They like to smile and make others laugh as you can tell right from the first announcement.

Microsoft hires super smart problem solvers. Their initial recruiting questionnaire is often over 100 pages when completed by an applicant. If you don't love solving problems, Microsoft is not the place for you, because your job will be an endless stream of them.

Patagonia hires people who are passionate about being in the outdoors and believe in "Going Easy on the Rock" a metaphor for Planet Earth. Employees ride their bikes to work, tend the rooftop garden, recycle everything and spend a lot of time volunteering for environmental causes.

Can you see that these employees are NOT interchangeable? Can you imagine a Microsoft programmer on his or her 8th trip of the day as a Southwest flight attendant? Can you imagine a Southwest flight attendant after a week alone in their cubicle? Now that you are clear about your brand and your OverPromise, make sure that you only recruit those people who are strong believers in your message, purpose and cause and are Aligned with your business model. Recruiting to your brand is critical to your success.

Filter Every Decision Through Your OverPromise

Every action by every employee must be pulled through the filter of the OverPromise. "Does this action Align with our OverPromise?" "Does this action amplify, reinforce and prove our OverPromise?" If not, don't do it. If it does, ask how you can do it on steroids.

Drive Brand Culture Relentlessly

Culture is what employees do AUTOMATICALLY. If you are constantly driving your OverPromise message, both internally and externally, you will soon see that a set of automatic behaviors starts to drive the organization on a relentless quest to fulfill it, align with it and OverDeliver on it.

Even though you are the one who started this process, you'll be surprised and amazed one day when one of your team questions a long-standing practice or new idea on the table. They will be doing exactly what you've asked them to do, to filter every decision for fit with your OverPromise. And they will be right! Don't automatically dismiss them because of their position, personality or your conviction about the idea or process.

Stop. Listen carefully, and then make the decision that most aligns with your OverPromise. That's the moment when you'll know the right culture is finally taking hold. The next generation of believers has been born...and that is what will carry your company, product and brand into a very profitable future!

Conclusion

I hope you've enjoyed your journey through the Alignment process and understand why it is The Shortcut to Marketplace Dominance. Rather than spending years trying to manage every TouchPoint and chasing random strategies, you now understand that getting the entire team focused on just a few TouchPoints can turn your fortunes in very short order. Many companies that have been in business for decades never have this level of clarity and their bottom line shows it. They muddle along but somehow never break out in reputation, revenues or profitability. They never breakout in their contribution to their employees, customers and their communities, either. They get by…but they really don't make a difference in the world.

Step Up

You are different. You want something different. I know that because you are still reading. The losers gave up after the first chapter. You want to make the biggest contribution you can make to your employees, your customers, your community and to your dreams. You want to build a company that you can be proud of. You are a true entrepreneur who knows how to create real value and lead your company to real success. You understand true Alignment.

Take Action

Now that you've read the book in its entirety, it is time to take action. It's time to gather your team together and start at the beginning with step one. Follow the process as outlined. We've been perfecting it for over a decade. Let us know how you are faring and feel free to email your questions or success stories. I can be reached at rick.barrera@barrera.com

Have Fun!

Alignment projects are some of the most fun projects I've ever worked on. They are collaborative and customer focused and really profitable. Don't forget to have an enormous amount of fun building an extraordinary company while taking care of your customers in ways they never thought possible. There should be smiles all around!